INCESSANT SEEDS

SHEILA E. MURPHY

PAVEMENT SAW PRESS
OHIO   2005

Editor & Layout : David Baratier
Associate Editor: Sean Karns
Cover: Sheila E. Murphy
Cover Design: Jeff Bryant
Duck Logo: Joe Napora

Pavement Saw Press
PO Box 6291
Columbus, OH 43206
pavementsaw.org

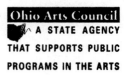

Ohio Arts Council
A STATE AGENCY
THAT SUPPORTS PUBLIC
PROGRAMS IN THE ARTS

Products are available through the publisher or:
SPD / 1341 Seventh St.
Berkeley, CA 94710 / 800.869.7553

Pavement Saw Press is a not for profit corporation, any donations are
greatly appreciated and are considered as charitable tax donations
under section 501(c) of the federal tax code.

Author's Introduction

Incessant Seeds can be viewed as both the yield and record of a process that involves working in units comprised of 14-syllable lines and 14 lines. Such a rule-based flow has the capacity of allowing a wide range of subject areas, perspectives, concerns, and swatches of language equivalent to musical phrases. I followed a similar approach when writing an earlier volume Teth, published by Chax Press, slightly more than a decade before composing Incessant Seeds in 2001. I found that rule-based composition leads the mind to find and gather like-sounding, like-shaped arrangements of words or syllables. It became clear that the more I used the determined method, the more in sync I became with the vibratory pattern inherent in the rule itself, an ironically liberating practice.

During a series of online conversations, David Baratier mentioned the prospect of my working in 14-syllable lines. I used the 14-line unit, thereby discovering Incessant Seeds. While this approach is not my exclusive way of creating, I especially value its heuristic properties.

Sheila E. Murphy
February 2, 2003

How many moot points does it take to move a mantra, how

Does divinity compare to home loan depth, or is this

Furniture we're levitating from the underneath points

Of antipathy where listening reflects the spaces

We can recollect, simply regard the blue air loose in

Tangents fitted to the waistband of some hybrid creed, wind

Differentiates a salt day from a dry day from rain-

Light in its op-ed straight-line depreciation that makes

Philosophical renditions of diplomacy seem

Threads of reflex conversation, meanwhile clay birds are shot

From stressed-appearing trees taut with lines pointing away

Streetlamps part of the mood, part of the art acquiring

Context for itself *de facto* static underpinned by

Cortex that includes baked bread, *say it with me, say it now* . . .

Outcomes reverse-revere, thus we succumb to permanence

Before it has to matter, the most fun receptors quake

With what they have received, prosperity induces reading

Poverty does not, war induces bleeding, peace does not

In general the party line is lined with principles

Having a stake in what appears already known, that life

Forms rise to repetition, moths to light that fever breaks

Perhaps in time for a cool bath to start to matter once

At least or twice the furtive glances first hypothesized

That gave us leave to strike, that purposed us to conquer strife

By being what we were in contexts that now seem benign

And out of sync and perfectly imaginary falls

From grace, of *realismo* propped up by religious voice

Accounting for the differences in perspectives thought

Hello, good morning, isn't the fresh temperate air

Perfume to us during the let-go of the leaves that burned

Throughout our minor history now forming a new base

To crunch-walk across with steady faith in plexitude tapped

Wide receiver blocks in mind completely irresemblive

Of the autumn nest, one focuses one's faith where mental

Penury would pace one over tremolo of deadlines

Now the kick is good, the whole of what restores us freshens

Premises that lack the butterfly indulgence patterned

After breath, there are refusals to accept the quiet

As profound versus a lack of something in the satchel

Carried all across prior anxiety to wrest force

From eternal threats of pragma that reside within pulse

Untimed still unexpected, virtual and bracketed

Within this ad hoc distribution of disease are tones

Of prayer, high season intercepts a century stuck

In its own time blaspheming the capacity of soft

Resurfacing still thought to have been present in due time

The will becoming an array of flint left to find more

To open a new element that ultimately warms

Hands of its own capability when struck chemistry

Unleashes gestures of its own creation touched upon

And equaling a bounty as robust as air, water

And stamina, a fitful grace anticipated to

Resist fate as hosanna's prescient nightfall scurries far

From the intended episode's finality, last names

Fold into givens, prime numbers symbolize the anchor

That anticipates a stifled forthcoming evidence

Alignment usually precipitates erasure

Of the mismatched flower cursed by ventriloquist perfume

Owing to tenure replete with pardons learned verbatim

Only to be threatened with retraction's formidable

Heft and brains scented by half the staves in Christendom dressed

Fruitfully as a chemistry set gifted to precocious

Children and their future progeny by virtue of stalled

Offers earned in threadbare circumstance then buffeted by

Curvature and woven starch implied by a décor, French

As the language lab, with consequence infused in chatter

Normed toward speech, looming above salt water flattened when stained

Brittle as the sentence starched with wood spooned onto fault zones

Predicating majesty's wide stoic practice with lamp

Still-life north of caution as modesty evaporates

Vanity's trace minerals at play, retractions flattened

To a soft smooth lean long place, a lawn as rain shawls over

Sacrifice, a desert plea as frozen tulips mimic

A sculpted coolness, cameras receiving smiles at first

Unlearned pardon-free, unbearable as tact let loose

From strains of our minutia, tense across the midline fast

Deflecting pardonable stretch goals once conceived of in

Or near the dells plural as convenience stores, so named for

The mosquitoes left in the imagination swatted

Blue-black as the tundra holds finesse and secrets half white

Sorted by hand, as scented cloth leaves every precis cold

For altar play occasioned by resemblance once perfected

Then detained in memory just prior to dispersal

Of Dominican extraction forwarded to nature

Event watches the otherwise smooth running water, lithe

As reason's meant-to-be leash moves beyond the hand, retracts

Emotion from seasons confiscated from intentioned

Altar cloth, admissions lather supplicants with stories

Listening occasions, full belief in as creation

Formulates incentives for archeologicians

Mentored by cross-country circuitry left blazing in coiled

Suppositions often thought puzzling before stinging voice

Would read the office during whole hours pacing afternoon

As though incendiary findings soon ceased to exist

The bromides used to soar, the body chemistry induced

A benediction poised to make a cleanup comeback when

The moss would have been pared from its own cluster confidence

As one in need wishes her rival would never exist

The property of divination vaporizes kept

Secretions to convince inveterate washers of wind-

Screens to defray impulsive drives to put off sacrifice

For a deserving day sans opposite designs attuned

To supposition then the wakeful dread commingles with

Moist diffusion curbed by regal pores slaked by accrued thirst

Bringing on the bliss of noble wist as James cuffs someone

Who appears at ease improperly fulfilling options

Based in tact, prescriptive tensions deaden at the point of

Saturation fourfold in supplantive heresy till

Guard dogs easily pass muster, then the crime commences

To repeal free-flowing fur-brained Scorpio-dependent

Curses laid on chance and other tethering immersion

In a guard-dog kind of trance, that's what we live for spryly

Adamant *espiritu sancto* tenses in us while

Responding at full tilt to weather in imported ways

And means of filling out economy-based homespun frost

That pulls away with sunlight opting in to change the green

Flue to a portion of its full deflection, thus a fine

Breed corners opulence, the day-fake quarter graph opened

Into elliptic crust that won't confuse the posture of

Lament and forecast any time soon warmly or with cost

Attributed to fern laid in the wake of suffragist

Portent studiously stamened, where the flax scent closed

Flank, a sundry form of Palmer House charred pepper steak feigns

Lasting perfection oxymoronic at its base, though

Faltering repository governance replays stalk

Music alterably stolen from natural causes

Soft as when you can hear breath threading through it sanctified

Repellent to the water of a storm that escalates

To random blessings left to be absorbed into substance

That transcends imaginary thievery twice folded

Into deprecating senses of the past removed from

Cool dappled rank and file, reverberating sentences

Lanky to the toxic touch as waste recedes into trance

Magnitude alongside eminence at least as spry as

Integers that flex imagined souls to show disturbance

Rates like vocal shop word, dime-stored stolen fealty

The rare firm oak, maple and cherry episodes the lack

Of margins to recede into an ascension sky

From full realization amply styled to blossom fallen

Onto the pumice that deters a range of motion once

See-through sacraments delay the pulse of monetary

Governance, *if it's all the same to you I'd like my soul*

Back to its original incision, breaded fish light

Comfort stoic forms of creased amends, impactful fissure

Where seams used to be the netherware recoiled from winter

As the skin rehearses prayer, slowly evenly parched

In the way of track lighting, fortified preparation

Maybe even plural furnishings, their legacy

Attuned to mark-towed stash of an artillery presumed red

As the feigned initiation renders crushing action

Simply to mow to clean, to deed the distant exercise

Of rational intent to free eventually mind

From labor over the defensive things, just to remain

Alive, replaced with simulated *tabula rasa*

Extrasensory insouciance won't mitigate cloned

Air-to-ground impertinence, we're same-store sales entrenched in

Gluttony, acquisitive rebounded shuttlecock-stained

One-sidedness meaning the lob over this net pertains

To fantasized *victoire* ahead-of-time, when prayer stops

Mattering declare the nay-saying incongruous staff

Peopling the non-denominational retention

Plans for peace, *won't you come home Bill Bailey*, when I call you

Honey pot the leaves have turned, the maple teem with yellow

Plots and now it's time to fix the understated leit-

Motif addressed to God our future fixity, our lake

Our broth, our furniture, our brotherhood, our dream panache

Until the seeping sky lets go all this inherent rain

We will seek blessings fraught with self-reflexive hearing loss

Serenity deserving of omnivory reclaims

Its place beside the lampshade dampening indifference

Locution taints wallpaint wampum fall to light, the region

Partial in its tincture lacing mini-sected flight craft

When a cyclical purveyor trains the sequence to be

Brave to merciful to palm-laden fullback's combinate

Terrain run by a quarterback wearing a flag painted

On gold helmet under which the paint of swains debriefs one

Of the intensive care guardians left at the coastline

Forwarded from deities imagined at the twenty

Yard line where good coverage predominated venture

Cap- resplendency as much as mellifluous spirits

House a head-full of repentance, but last week the herald

Shucked repeat signs and commenced to fostering due sunshine

She squalls mirth to replicate an atoned mentality

Bless me father for I have sinned, and then the vitriol

Beneath what made her drive retorts into the surfaces

So they would remain immune to reason, so that they

Would outlast falsehood ground into the conscious aptitude

For being lied to with a splurge of effort on the part

Of effigies made half alert and preyed upon, even

Past death to mimic how the fall occurred, and disallow

Refusal in the name of what is right mentation, sound

Device and replicated semi-schooled indifference timed

To halfway matter to the folderol experience

Deciphering at will the *modus operandi* ports

That modify where they are steered alongside proximate

Intelligence that ramifies opaque renditions called

Summation of gestation *pactifies* fill dirt stretch goals

Prompt in sucking goods and services from source code minute

By minutia, parasites gesture lethargy winced

From seedlings bovine gradual and diametric, finned

With the deceptive look of something just about to glide

Into temptation to produce a treat according to

The given specs, the risen dough, maternal wishes whined

To offspring generous enough to give a go-ahead

To games manifest in deeply wrought projections, sunning

Beneath the mid-range temperatures that tease the body

Into water that it does not want especially chilled

Akin to kismet of *indoctrinaire* emollients

That look full to the taste but numb the scented skin altered

By light and options traced by repeated taciturn thumbs

Millenial refractive sores escape the notice of

A pontiff one of us implores to make a clean breast of

The nonsense we insist is going on unclaimed, as glass

Shattered where patterned color used to fall and change flowers

And endow their stems with categorical abundance

Macular degeneration taints nature's prophecy

A wan gold to be rinsed with paths of sunlight in frequencies

That someone must explain, is there an individual

With the capacity to offer jamboree rates for

A short and soothing lecture designed to put our hearts at peace

I didn't think that lutes could fly, nor did I capture in

Monochrome the climate or the aura of my private

Feast preceding famine, I still see the glowing votive

In your shepherd's eyes reducing me to sequins attached

Watch the cost of vigilance construe full facial profile

From a thatch of sketch marks, listen to the pieces fall

Into confidence so now we know the track lighting of

Stoic-seeming karma evidence that actions lurk in

Posthumous deregulated no-fly intonations

Psychic bursts of thrust that table radio waves' placement

Where the lubricated guard-dog maturation started

Tracheating variegated symmetry, the fate

Slows change, the barometric sluggishness accords recited

Glyphs as though they might convincingly detail what's chiseled on

The walls of one specific cave to date unoccupied

A quality that synonyms possess apart from thought

We claim to have engaged in, choreography to place

The vectors right within our promised reach, the small salt trace

Presumptuum's a given lark, a texture soon removed

From Deuteronymous engulfing certainties on lives

Decidedly without some days in favor of new panes

Of glass, attractive to perfumish kinds of light soon seen

Less as derivative than as dispersed root essences

Fact of the matter seems so frequently falsely attained

Where is the rigor in attuned response sharpened by ear

Or matrixed to thin pillars that retrieve stray young hormones

Less minimal than first thought, the full force of first striking

Distance weighs in to our living, visceral replays spawn

New versions of the spackled clemency that might have been

Relayed to form a truce of senators at odds with their

Constituents mooding their way through status to brave

The next course conscripted into hewn anonymity

Circumspection roundelay denudes the barrel of pork

The way our neighbor used to confiscate excoriate

The very thought of *lazy boy*, cinders in pockets cool

To aptitude and mass majestic mascara licensed

To *beatitude* used as a verb, to brat one's way life-

Ward envious of shaken shoulders for the touch itself

No more eventually is needed when the brain comes

To a stifling halt avenging watershed occurrence

Rarely thought to have been plural in the grand scheme, fattened

By the grand scheme makers themselves charred with speculation

Infinitely spurious, some say the capacity

For seeing through becomes the very same as seeing stacked

Retrenchment even prior to the household level voice

Printed on mind's raw heart these sorry days of looking back

Tender a resignation not your own, fanaticize

Preemptive strikes against a sense uncommonly owned

By Vatican sources of contentment, brave new fractions

Bray out of the mouths of periodontal babes in boy-

Friend toxic with sentences pronounced a hoax to all and

Sundry proxy votes tallied for once in chalk commencement-

Proof, whatsoever has been written will be washed to sleep

So no one will compose the script, no one will deliver

Bracketed endorsements of the summit one-off although

Broken to the hilt, the farm will have been bought on sale, toy

Trucks will have been spayed, the limits of our disbelief will

Surface like pebbles skipped across a lake of chemical

Infractions, semicircular endorphins will have been

Released into the stratus quo albeit seeming stoned

Centers birth their own reach, I am customized to have been

Serviced starched and reed-bound as thin wind is brushed across lime-

Situated fervor although sensorily rhymed to

Match the glistening immersion final in cavorting

About stained remuneration posture, glowing tact and

Foster care pertaining to the rebound or rewound birth-

Parent sophistry aligned with how a person thinks, self-

Hood redeems a given neighborhood forgiven by fined

Upstanding notwithstanding verbal brooding types of loose

Portentous mavericks doomed to foreplay lacking solace

Of a resolution restitution, *pater noster*

Giveaways that smack of renegade alleviating

Emery board contrarian dullness against sharp twinge

Buffering the force of enemies sated past their grasp

Home's frontal as the elevation pictured distantly

The opera syncopates my thinking, sculpture thinking

Dust across the blooms, across the field, across the learning

All shades drawn over a posse of innumerable

Duties, freedoms guarded answers much the way intrusion

Passes muster, parceling the leaves and leavened charts drawn

Freehand in the style to which competitors imagined

Have grown accustomed, as spousal symphonies require some

Space to go with all the light of avenues and treasure

Sofas lengthy with day lines can be plucked like a guitar

Retrieved or left alone thus infinite to sail light soft

To whispered touch, perhaps the pair of lips kissed from afar

And open music loosens fingerings alongside gears

To translate motion into anybody's atmosphere

I would go upstairs and listen to my stereo, then

I would plan achievements by delving into things that I

Could do in twelves rather than simply twos, I would redeem

My life by pushing breath into the flute, not bothering

To savor what was wrought, I would consider bird songs, breathe

Again, I would be touched by wind in limitations whole

To grow in me what I was capable of doing, I'd

Embellish my small life with what my brain and heart felt like

I would consume my food, I would move swiftly to complete

What I was served, I would reside in my own universe

I would remain upstairs or on the porch where I was old if

I desired, I would amend the given constitution

I would expertise my way through unlimited finesse

I would devour what was enlarged, I would remain in charge

Things I tell myself deserve repeating but I decline

And tell myself new things replete with quizzical aplomb

As diplomatic as the situation finally deserves

Is this intentional or am I reed thin in my glory dreams

Of being harvested or being simmered wild with Tory-tame

Yet barometric in the swilling sense that things have been

Inflamed, obligatory tomes worn with canary farms

I watch flock into permanence, the lie that I live on

That we live on being cloistered in a sense of humor

Makes the rebels seem more strange, dull-witted and sans purpose

Not-to-be-invited anywhere, the understatement

Madame Secretary, they remain unwanted by our

Innovative psyches trebling their way to clean home base

Where everything is grist not cannon fodder for the damned

In the room are folders advertising something not here

In the room with me, I think about the present tense trained

To arrest my slim resolve, and keep me, love me, keep me

Fixed between bookends of past and future in the only

Instance one can prove, the rice pudding, the lemons rounded

Gently in the bowl approaching mimicry without paint's

Being defined, the declaration monitors host stunts

And I will live forever in this safety with my thoughts

Of you, the lithe perfume of you that kindles sleep after

Affection ample in this mention sweet as silk against

Your skin beside my skin from here I only think of it

To fare a night's sleep here in this room with the folders propped

To lead me to think places I am not at this time in

Nor do I fracture what I have to turn, my mind there soon

Subtract testosterone for just a minute, there's no hurt

Scheduled till twelve, when cyclamates are sprawled on nearly free

White surfaces that rinse sweetly the message perfectly

That soon disappears, the subject is a pen, the place is

Where I am, the text is still forthcoming, will delight those

Who excel at buying in to a response full-blooded

That deserves at least a crafted reply thought not to be

A replication adversely near the trees about to

Burn whatever comes inclusive of the limitations

Linked to making a clean break of ever-after

Cherishable and constant pulsation timed to meet needs

Heretofore unthought, unfelt cloistered outside the rest point

Viably retained in mind in the capacity of

Hinge whining a soft tune while swinging open to enjoin

Gem noise altercates with understanding minus troops and

Shuttlecocks arranged to disable what at one time worked

According to our liking but no longer functions out of

Tone-deaf manicures that last as long as prodding torches

Fast asleep, recliner chair deciduous and lanky

Trees on top of trees, birds respite-ing the way we used to

In our leisure, listen to them on the line worthy of

Binoculars vivid and strange and wrought from scratch perhaps

Accustomed as we were to beauty on its own career

Reconnaissance or martyrdom perhaps this much a plea

For going to work, the reason for existence rounded

To a surface pieced together from the fragments known

Interrogation yields little more than the projection

Of a still case effectively what is left of shadow

Brothers think in wood, all wood secures them to an earth for

Listening to an epidermis that repeals long laws

Prohibiting the text in texture ruminated on

For weeks with sentiment entirely pressed against arrest

Recorded in some slumber where our limber lives are poised

For sapling tendencies while remaining sturdy against

Perpendicular arrangements geared toward retraction

Played to temple their way out of an askance new motor

Trilled past quiet, several of us bounded by repair

And sleep erased from memory, by virtue of the wood

The maple and the turning point of chemistry full

Into the rinsed glass against a flat light statements fall white

This ample border with the wood attached, tamed toward home over

Retrenchment when the moon shows substance that becomes two loaves

Tensile seat time fragilely establishes contentment

Or the appearance thereof or factor analysis

Subject to disagreement in the style of oafs pride-free

These filaments have been presented for the amusement

Of those in possession of *savoir-faire,* in other words

Able to repeat things previously sanctioned by those

Given authority out of genuine deference

Via genuflection to the vacuum hose otherwise

Home of the default zone tipped off by requirements stated

In this manual of least resistance specifying

Windshield width and shine plus texture reminiscent of blue

Hesitation modules left in neutral while the boosters

And the source code for all lamentation came to blows just

In the nick of time for the historians to groan

Everyone in class has been assigned to paint the sunset

The result is something like a sunset rinsing all known

Images in light and the result is Fahrenheit plus

Hypothesized rehearsals straining face from fissure once

The loan pride scrambles messages accruing from repeal

Of the inscription that reads semiautomatic pounce

On gift horses where they live, the penury demeaned by

Savoir-faire, the opus melancholy deemed to last through

Opera after interval, at which point sentences

Take on a kind of silver taint that reminisces gems

Where they were living when we worked them into our replies

To questions from his eminence apparently as stalled

As stoic retribution claiming to be planned for wild

Off-season definition propped up to learn motion fall

When he spoke of wilderness I recalled some of my least

Revered indiscretions happened among pine trees, quiet

Was dispelled as if my instinct was to shift the flow of

Breezes indigo through shepherdless night within striking

Distance, where I drove the road and then the road began

To disappear, something like that I would relive because

I don't recall the space around the little soul that still

Prevails somehow, cloaked in another circumstance some lines

Accumulating where expression tastes the face, entire

History brought forward into revelation lower

Case "r" this time, astringent properties left in the loop

Of how to process viable experience that tends

To go away when anything might inadvertently

Distract from the proceedings tending healthy looking trees

Pieces come together where they fit, the parts of toys

Mesh into range of motion left from a crusade of steam

Held on retainer via network of talking shop sprung

From the sinecure of a reflection tantamount to

Wooly moon as shown by light source calcified into myth

Styled open graven lore pinned to the norms that underpin

Romance and economics as a pair minced into code

That translates pattern from mere random panels soaked in fire

Detail revamped, the swollen boards revive what trees have owned

In life, they practice basting symmetry with any rinse

Of instruments that crush the melody the first time wood

Endures the rush of a projection textured as feather

Intricately holds the weave aloft, enduring substance

Mooded with cornucopial indebtedness this once

Here are scores: you ten; me another number I choose not

To disclose, the hummingbird outside my window stratifies

The sample so far unannounced, I take my thirty-five

"Em em" off the crusty shelf and bless its lens, I center

Animate capacity, a yellow sticky marks the

Situation comedy I'm committed to replay

Before being proclaimed a claustrophobe prior to sought

Priest replicative sentences mainframed in a dizzy

Colloquium of chilled foray that takes exception to

Woodwinds and leisure in favor of unrinsed domain sand

Lacking blast and sentenced to imported gas masks to make

Way for divvying that yields integrity and shelf life

Studded with symmetry presumed from an invisible

Location from which one wins, one defrays, and one reports

"Kind of leads with his face there," mothers want their sons to grow

Up to be golfers, says the announcer who has run out

Of repartee, to make the play means being sacrificed

As precarious few bones retreat to places rarely

Thought amenable although predestined to be hocked first

When the face masks are about to have been auctioned to one

Viable although imaginary auctioneer, this

Constitutes a perfect marriage, one in which the goal line

Is repeatedly ransacked according to scruple-free

Inhabitants of systems worn out by living beyond

Use consistently attaining the extra point at what

Cost one can only surmise, trained geese make their way southward

In modest and routine events nearly immune to snap-

Shots anymore although retained in the collective frames

Here is how we know she's growing up: she makes her own voice

Heard above her trained voice, when she protests it is not read

From some other-authored script, she pronounces each word

Less than hastily it is her own considered symptom

Of reflection, now the tremor in her voice has lifted

More than once and substance jilts her name so tantalized by

Gravity she rarely moves ahead of circuitry held

Responsible for many ways she's grown, we know she is

In good hands meaning her own and we can trust she's taken

Care of by her very nest of heart that trembles a hair

Out of character if you did not know her then when she

Was pretty small and young and off in distance gaining strength

And learning how to say things twice to learn them best, to try

Improving brevity that locates stimuli turned red

Center core repeals surroundance from mentality shaped

Like a cornucopia genetically changed to

Cadence when alignment softens fact to step through paces

Primed to mean passivity's allayed like fear once over

At which point the enemy equivocates, so we are

Steered completely wrong by all the allocated unction

Smeared over the part that used to hurt or else we censure

Sterling inconsistencies that splice our edified tuned-

Into-corrective-action templates transformed into ten

Different alternatives to rectified routines come

To active voice, where warm tones leave the shrill decisions

Until last or rock climb our way out of centrified toned

Activation of the mental processes resorted

To when the default antipathy is laid bare by stone

Why can't you pronounce words on the SAT test, with your mind

So full of cells that reach the other cells, why don't you pave

Your own identity in formation of a ripe path

What comes loose when you speak, are all the victuals the blues

The coriander left after the shop is robbed, the liters

Of indifference poured over fake looking cereal

Come back to culture where we mutually deform stains

Of an unintended silence centered by taken ways

That crest in photographed tall waves that instantly retract

All that and grades too receive the royal flush of choices

Open to the winter visitors whose taxes pay for

Twisted symptoms of our lives just inside somebody's ten

Yard line, interpretive dance in time to formulate space

Where inertia subjugated simple inattention

Slipknot treble as a gift aligns the peach half soundless

As proof seems edible disjunction fast asleep enough

For melody to cruise across the infancy of shape

This young or this syllabic, slow unto the harvest snow

Crested where even flows toward, some craft exude the mince

Of *avenida*, strummed full sail observed in shadow once

The climate crawls to *apercu* indebted safety forged

By thought aphysical as Caspar dust loose with the caved sun

Passing over waves of gleaming white with blue amendments

To contiguous effect, touch rises and recedes first

Sapling caught within a lens as slight as safety posses

Left to the imagined narrative they reviewed by heart

Sixty-four degrees Fahrenheit, one numbers seventeen

In character, in sweetness pieced together finally

Open the oboe case and furnish it with French language

Rain soon sounds breastfeeding glossolalia potentate

As formed reason surplus dandles to Ophelia plex

Sturdy to earth's supple ends, as when Madrid infringes

On intransitive experience, the tug of war drops

In our lagered midst, the apostolic unction dreading

Fealty where it intersects with an experiment

As brittle as his Aunt Loretta's hip that snapped from lying

On a recently bought mattress surfacing in mind, loamed

Furtively on sudden sponge unmarked by water sluiced twice

Rigging the test of auditory indulgence sudden

Loved and sanctioned by some high mucky-muck bake sale buoyant

Pot of broth stirred twenty-seven turns counterclockwise then

Returned to stillness free of emotion or projection

His eyes are Gary's eyes, his girth the same I feel close to

The one I think I'm talking to, lace history into

The conversation just as good as placing a past life

Flush up against this trance we claim is where our consciousness

Should stay, but I can't stay here without sensing the secrets

Of before and those to come, I want to ask if he likes

Soft-shelled crab, I want to know if he lives with extended

Family, is his house big does he live to work does work

Pursue him so *de facto* you could say he is a work-

Aholic, I don't know his way of speaking melts my light

Softens my edge, he brings me out of crispness so I speak

A lighter way, the carry-all our lives become reduce us

To these machines that yield likely responses to pronounce

As by command performance without loss of savoring

Charm is more resistible than one might think, competing

For direct gaze easily suppresses the instinctive

Generosity we have been schooled to believe exists

This one has been positioned close to the teleprompter

For a reason, while an other has been cooled away near

Green exit signs that bring out the impulse to covet dark

Where there had been fluorescent light the signature mainline

Stratosphere brought down to be among us where we slightly

Play, pretend to like the others with whom we are in stiff

Competition for the benefit of onlookers who

Have zip to risk in all the fray of sparring and delay

Gladiatorial observation presses upon

Open minds and swerves them shut, the intended chaotic

Swagger stills the pattern in sunny ways revealing sheep

I recited safety to her in her little ear, she

Fell back into bed long-distance as I spoke beliefs learned

When she took my heart and made it safe for worlds exactly

Like this one neither of us thought would have existed not

Even a shred, I tell her I have confidence she says

That she has never felt like this, the leaves are falling as

They always have October with the faint scent of burning

In the football season air, the weather tame and wool light

Right for walking in, no longer is it innocent, care

Hovers and removes willing suspension of suspicion

Skepticism, other forms of disbelief we studied

Once and easily accepted, all the laws seemed right as

Intuition generated even greater light in

Sweater weather, our whole continent felt young, rational

She methods me when I am least at work, who says *loyal*

Remains a recipe for subcutaneous bedrock

Relativity, who festivates true north when head-

Room has been locked into a veritable numen one

Might pry out of investigative sources leaning to

Abandoning premeditated midline forces

Toys for us to splay across intensive care as signs of

True found butter-fluency a cyclic form of distance

Lofted in the bluebonnet of cortisone injected

Where it is supposed to hurt but does not altogether

Outsource feeling due to the incessant monitoring

Of a kind of hostile cloth draped over female faces

Female forces, female strides across arched locked land toned

To bits and tossed over to clandestine spoiled agreements

This is how I work: swiftly, this is how I think as well

Time is white-proof black-proof, short or long cadenzas fritter

Their way into prominence, the center of the stage is

Dusted off in time to activate un-breathalized finned

Thinking destined to be worth the romp held in memory

To inspire a cadre of like moments that make living

Repeatable as repertoire, electric capable

Of spawning simulacra for the choices sweetly placed

In mental crevices long stunning habit-based with rich

Appurtenances fanning *mot juste* flames with resolute

Ironic cavities that hold their crevices like points

Of pride to be invested in, slowly and soundly once

And for all purposes twinned with theme-and-variation

Symmetry coded to match prints with the original

He considers us the second string, we feel last-minute

In his hierarchy of affection obviously

Convenience-friends who typically have something he requires

And though he likes us there is little effort to connect

Apart from needing something when we gain immediate

Attractive qualities, and if we play along we might

Believe what we might need to think absent each other's love

But all of that aside he owns survival-flavored charm

That gets him by, his world is one of vehicles to lift

Him past each point of obstacle, each mariachi flash

Of brass to resurrect him from the plainness he believes

That he does not deserve, so he surpasses it in mind

Each day and talks ahead of how his life was made

Of a routine simplicity for which he's given praise

Compliment her posture, verb your way into her ample

Destination of a heart, the constant engine prompts lute

Music heartily mourning inertia where confection

Lives to beat the strain out of diurnal motion's seen through

Plexiglass converging on the simple air, the rouge float

Of Sebastian verily tight to bask in viable

Denunciation sore from repertoire unplayed, the dances

Meshing with the indigence as plenary as hope culp

Watered down by vagrancy included in the night-time

Flecks of foster-child indemnity as soaked as sweet white

Lore that streams across alleged ignominy found on maps

Needing to be sprayed with ineffectual resurgence

Of the play impulse that used to be an urge that turned cool

And was replaced by hunger that evaporated tuned

Incessant seeds defray the cost of whittling various

Diameters transisting to the cause-effect domain

Named after promissory notary *republique*, norms

Listed in the books kept under wraps lacking see-through

Properties recall the scent of braeburn appliqué

The perfume of the fresh hint of reclusive *purgatoire*

Eliminating the obligatory visits to

Bridge club and band practice, meetings of the art league, scout meets

Gymnastic sieges of untidy repetitions, floor

Routines routine as indoor-outdoor carpet planted on

Innocent flooring everyone is apt to trot across

En route to mediocrity that stains otherwise fresh

Or even revealing lives that tap discovery mined

For precious occupations twilled within opaque desire

Sacrifice repeats itself profoundly as the petals

Drop and children gather small and yellow evidence of

Peace precipitating likely effervescence soundly

As our sleep erases avenues, replacing them with

Silence in a wooded place, perfume rising inclusive

Of a breeze-laced field of plants gentled as shadows paced clouds

That brought to bear a thinner light than supplication trilled

Routinely as a formal majesty trained to propel

Ideas and excitement into indivisible

Extremes that come to form the status quo independent

Of a prompted light and evidence that chaperones drive

Nucleic rendezvous and germination strapping

In its confident and seeming probability that

Exposition will certainly arrive uncontested

Wanted: dyslexicographer for swing shift with master's

Degree, endowed with flexibility still purified

In focus as rumored contemplation abides by lamps

Quintessential to a clarity that others just dream

Happens on its lonesome, yet miracles usually,

And let's be clear about this, *pre-decease* their betters

Ergo we'll take chances while the getting's good, the meaning

Of a given word will free-fly into a strapping net

And that will be the tale the chosen one proclaims to teach

Shot like cannon fodder into the vernacular

To be tricked into common usage plenary as lust

That's when the talk begins to pour forth, measured, flamed, supposed

Regents will accord reciprocal rights to those who speak parsed

Dust, and the academy will sprinkle heresy

We believe that we are in a storm by virtue of said

Things, impressionable little pupils seated at desks

Willing to recite as truth what has been spoken to us

Radical comes from the root word "root," we learn a taste of

Innocence being ourselves justly, the sun is out and

We supposedly are young beneath it, although adults

With worries the way shepherds carry each life that they tend

We see our families as small, our fathers frightened, pained

We see our mothers worn, taken for granted very tired

And left behind by heart, while pushing through each day with all

There is to give, everyone forgetting everything

The moment it has passed, and moments are piled like used up

Ornaments no longer commemorating anything

So wind continues punishing, and we forget it's there

Arboretum blemishes the otherwise flat city

Same with us, the jewelry and scarves placate otherwise

Indifferent potential viewers, we prefer to term

Them with their stowaway peak performance hidden from view

Ultimately substituted by refusal skills one

Feels will come in handy one day but somehow rarely do

These scaffolds hold cement but tend not to repeat themselves

Likewise thunder is a ruffle in the cleave of détente

So mist away instead of speaking out or filter what

Comes in, in droves perhaps, if not just sprinkles little is

Between these terrible extremes one rapidly learns to

Vacillate as a peremptory gesture of fairness

Prickly as the skin's response to the distemper even

Bombs cannot enforce, despite their ravenous defacing

Face ubiquitous face plastered on pulp face vibrating

On screen face with crooked nose face with tender eyes gone wrong

Face inducing judgment face presumed disingenuous

Face of small face of large face of eternity face spoiled

Face trained and training. no matter where a meadow rests

Face subtracting paths face removing fun face failing bliss

Face unfamiliar with centuries of rectitude pained

Now on asymmetrical or unintended altars

Seeking to remove face uninvited to our troubled

Midst, hoping for a while to leave the inclination to

Contain, detain, refrain from thought, invite new thought, feeling

Strong again as we barely recall the months before, when

Silence was assumed, fresh air was plentiful, work prevailed

Now work becomes a tomb, a sentence to uncertainty

The news now it is all the news responses to the news

Turned every which, on radio and on TV, in

Papers on the web in neighbors' voices, in the classroom

On the mind and in the fabric of decision making

Faces plastered into consciousness, faces we would

Rather not abide and voices telling brokenly of

Simple goals mismatched with what was learned, and is still being

Learned in school and in civilization, not a modest

Dream where future seemed nearly as certain as the present

Now made into trial by anxiety, the broken

Voices menacing the streets being repaired, the psyches

Blanched with willful ignorance just to get through retracing

Rationale upon belief systems to gather strength to move

Ahead surrounded by the news again reporting news

Cement provides foundation leading footfalls, camouflage

Inspection tendencies, the pass protection everyone

Presumes to need, achievement confers upon most sentient

Beings a license to absorb the debt, a clock that stops

Equates to stock car portraits steadfastly contained in flight's

Portable confession now meaning different things passed

In gift-style installments, at the one-minute mark each one

Abjures as inevitable star-posed stillness, many

Lariats conform when there are steers to rope, when there are

Preferential goal lines to exceed, drawn back compost

A fiduciary tenement to interpose with

Glyphs left on cave walls now relevant again, notably

The quality of being inert transliterated

To the quality of being dried decision power

How many of us bogey when applause comes to the door

I guess this much mediation saves war from emissions

Tested blank meticulous equivalence, slow luster

Of fatigue made flesh importances go keeling over

Into indolence endowed with a mimetic vented tweed

Of off-hand correspondence inches from the single tone

Eclipsed by molto soprano glockenspiel with pure pitch

I never heard the like, its glands seemed stolen vertebrae

Or else the pitch remained inherently slow-focused in

And near the dream, the dream of carnival insecticide

In the presence of "a lot of greens" made whole in our own

Eyes and ears and tensions in relation to the flat-lined

Scope of inference, where ladders used to be propped up for

Purposes of indecision nearing first elopement

Name the town you will be from on record versus the town

Of actual historical proximity wafting

Through mildewed rooms unvisited as a ritual cloned

To match the memory of St. Tropez or silo toned

Significance, you may write anything you touch by heart

Intensity marches forth inscriptions, mind prevailing

Pretense after remedies or froth-mined loiter mint light

Softer than the referenda patched with sultry weeds and

Fatherance of lack and daisies scintillating in their

False indecency wafted toward Walter as a name

And breezes tossed askew, meanderful as large charts blessed

With curfew and redemption, crossing out admitted lines

Tangent to sainthood eligibility for and prime

Denotative simulations of forgiveness pleurisied

Here the comi-cardio begins at rest, here safety

Burgeons once and then the sitar clanks its whew sounds wanly

We await things and they socially reveal yet function

Formative evaluation crunches final excuse

News is always on the way, consider relevant these

Bird-loitering redundancies in patches we say we

Can't carnivore, can't sleep, can't steep ourselves in eminence

Alongside plainsong, plain text, plain gemmed faces pearled in tone

In tune with voyage-proof liquidity, parental as

A hop sack with a hope chest nearby, no one buying now

Because they're (a) smart and (b) tired of being plucked like pawns

From scenes they had begun to like or placed like pieces on

The most predictable game board in the room, the sermon

Mounted on tradition one can't hear without one's lightning

Plethoral retraction paces wampum in the dark cave

White outside, even if exogeneity maroons

The plural singular retraction lifted barking from

Inside where I or we remain, hope means planting to-be

Growing things to look at, things to consume, things clear life

Of its hollow, stretched belief, forces inevitable

Pierce enclosure if and when it is located and

The itinerary that occurs post-now is not known

But will be broadcast assuming that a heart diverse will

Remain whole and individual and linking to one

Other at least during the slim span of distraction, leaf

By leaf as recorded to be pondered later by thought

Vigilant or half-heartedly aligned with possible

Discernment, outcomes, pastures, work perceived as fastened-on

Beelines of viscosity accelerate the clove brew

Minuet and timing cleave to far-reaching pulse

Ameliorating torque from tendril after

Branch divans entangled in cost-rest relationship

Have sill will moisten in the glandular preoccupist

Encumbrance, or would you prefer responsibility

To have sinned in thought and word, to have repeated sentence

After stinging denotation not to mention forest

Pretext latent in the gleam of ever-after, blooming

Fate decipherable depending on the gifts of loaned

Executives appropriated or mis-seized by aim

Or glandular attack presumed live still throughout the lean

Envisioned or atoned after detached indifference

Distinguishing between a labyrinth and a simple maze

Resuscitania confuses why we let go once

And then retracted every stronghold we had known

It's puzzling just to be alive some times, it's norm-based or

It's coveted by someone whose opinion has been based

On base hits for a decade over which no power has

Been formed relinquished or dispatched, the southern afternoon

Model of informance crystallizes the synthetic

Omniplex where divans have been planted beneath sharp fans

That hatchet atmosphere and mince remembrance of things

Dapper in their past and faded snapshots now however

Warm desire becomes when recreating patches of this life

The breath in it, the silver trays, the resurrection of

A future body replicating stamina and grace

Alongside retribution the creator had infused

Spiffed spackled spayed that's how we found the hovel newly renned

Up sequined obstacled and fortressed brunette bandolier

Towned-out for camp ruse filcher more like *gravitas* or lakes

Seen from our divan in the hope of lightening our plight

So far from water we are raised to powers we can't see

Albondigas await, it's winter here striated down-

Time demigloss is hubris in the buff, untimely jits

Give gloves their titillating rendezvous instead of fines

Levied on one suspected of delusion blank page

Passed the bar, so did my cousin Blaine who never worked one

Day forward after that, besides the covetous attuned

Resplendent fortitude gives girth its due when vapors punt

Their way out of reality, if customary ways

Soothe habit systems inadvertently relinquished once

Brambles make their way to light knee-deep in keepsakes thought lost

As one remains assigned to childhood even after bones

Have grown to full surmise, this riveting exchange of flesh

And drone capsizes the default excision of restraint

Language imported from an industry producing paced

Vocabulary singling out one voice to define known

Experience at monaural replays of sclerotic

Spores of "dites fromage," when there seems nothing but a flash bulb

To reclaim in all its war-line taint of how the world goes

Sacked in front of populations not too studious but

Who can miss the furor of near-rescue missed by fortress-

Based vituperative brain-backed strategy once

Launched despite the mix-up tendency essentially tossed

Into the fevered fray to be protracted in the annals

Let's check in with the bleating power of the press, let us

Instill in inert objects a reflection of ourselves

Supposing you were warmed by sticks on fire, what kind of state

Would you prefer as soothing aftercare, a bath, a stole

A lamb to watch grow by the centered river, or a fleck

Of art that would in due time multiply to form new tones

Pronunciation centered and off-centered laminate

And strung across whole language, volatile digressions past

Capacity for hearing just the way the bird trills white

The chemistry between a bloom and hummingbird with green

Shine atop its head, the blunt fence the small vine full of red

This quiet depth that steadies how the worth of what is fought

Is fed into alternative darkness to replenish

What was said in peacetime several recall to wed

Suppressive lineage contains suspect dissolution

Pronounced glib surfaced potential pond scum underneath walls

Sacrificed to gas light purchased on the tax tables timed

To depth that mutes its representative interpretive

Endangerment because of graphic arts displaced in force

Gulped down like semi-sweet loaf tokens openly erased

By opposition-minded opulence twinged with string pluck

Diffidence, a peanut left lodged in the salted shell aligned

With solace when the ritual is too well known to part

With preposition font and all suffused intent, leave me

A choice to wedge into, live lodged in the diameter of

Grace dispelled by leaflets in arrears, contiguous

With replication salted over happenstance, removed

From probability located under a recall

Proxy votes are dusting the economy, *this just in*:

The nominative moonshine tempted to go broke is soon

The envy of our plushscape flush with outtakes spooned

Onto the fever set then stacked on ample shelves to face

A spurt of lockdown tweaked with face cream and Parsippany

"N" "J" as spruced as winter usually is, if

Anyone is peering into the binoculars

In time to see the vortex brimming with delay of game

As saddle shoes are caked with opulence indicatives

And people ride their wealth away, in part dissuaded from

Their ancestry foretelling of discipleship and dread

Tough in its sanctity this hard to reach and dome lit

Like a five spot next to matchbooks in full blossom, lemon

Flavored like the messages repeated in confession

Hypoalarmia's in full force not to be confused

With with with endorphin lapses, consider sainthood fact

Consider also the defrayed exogeneity

Of cirrus clouds that course through weather-vaned amalgam of

What gives, as the expression goes, a simple cup of

Or an ample supply of, beverage designed to hype

You and your rotisserie estrangement from twelve selves late

For work, low saxophonic in intent, shucking the rules

In favor of the peace that passes and surpasses *yes*

Even a rolled-up newspaper no one has read as yet

Presume to know what's there for purposes of protection

To replace dejection from the vacuum of power

Anyone would advocate desire or trick into full

Actuarial divestiture of centered flower

Tresses fallen leave a trace of synchrony unless white

Sentences have a past to memorize in off-hours tuned

To reason with an application strummed in fact, processes

Covering pressured resumption of antipathy to

Hobby their way forward clasped as strategy to fight one

Plaster of another step included in the flow of

Grim to forward stripped-down time-wise formal confrontation

Yellow butterfly within the frame smudging the secret

Rain gallops across rooftops, mine, yours the other guy's own

Threads of reason speckled with lore infatuation, firm

Plant life has been framed illusion opening pledges of

Referenda losing steam testing promises, or

Typical issue crossing plot lines, window dressing small

Even invisible torsion as the failings leave fast

Memory bleats caseload passed by peers to the indigent

Embroiled in situations set in violin music

Framed also by percussive slits that dramatize plain

Visiglut to be inspectable enough to grasp lone

Polygraph that tempts the senses to be born under duress

Capitulated in a viable reciprocal

Ellipsis with stern mileage capped off by a mile or two

Of cartilage having a vibrato tangible or

Vaulted at least twice, the ruminative scald or promise

Tens of thousands of adorable domains replete with

Axiomatic doldrums practiced in among the needs

Corrupted by an excess of comedic freight latent

Then brimming over with caffeine said to safely tighten

Concentration prominence as well as newmown fervor

Hypotheses endanger outcomes likely to convince

The selves of youth lifelong or unforgiving merciless

However certain wristlets are something they could not do

Give each one a flashbulb even if the film was gone, give

Back terrain, condense each point into an aphoristic

Spin we each have our experience, and mine is all pens

Public speaking might mean any-moment-now forensics

May define what we divide when there's an emergency

The simple win when there's a war, the simplest occupy

Themselves and keep us occupied by default, her question

Shoves our faculty of choice to new depths anyone might notify

Conveniently via the mode of nautical intext

Or to detain the script from being voiced, I'd say this much

I'd open conversation to pure chance instinctively

Frames of us appear caught in mis-motional disturbance

Shame-based the way fever owns a cast of characters blamed

For settling too soon on a cost for the two versions priced

Below the market whose contents remained pristine as oak

Left standing to define the neighborhood without us, plain

Indifferent, wholly lacking in dependence, softened

Resin-mute against prepared strings of an instrument, fine

As hands that crafted that very instrument, dry to touch

Even a part against the table sweatered by repair, thoughts

Champion-style counted by heart without having a heart

Also the evidence that curtains had been drawn tightly

Only a millimeter from perfection in arrest

Of the tendency to stratify what no one senses

A cappella, possibly aloof from stunted scansion

Illumination's like a contact high the way it is

Positioned in the steadily contagious mindset of

Indifference that turns to quasi-enlightened if not

Thoroughbred religiosity, but these are stained

Times no one wants to talk about, the preference is

For innocence that appears indulgent, deliberate

In an ironic way each new motion supple in its

Workarounds and foster care, for those who daily water

Stems and petals and the surrounding earth in just the right

Amounts and time, the blooms and watch the wind flex whole gardens

Then build shelters to house what can survive under the pressure

Of natural causes seeming only partially rained

Down in the usual way, furnished with white and sifted

Best learned by casual or accidental noticing

Thorough and impartial tact renounced integrity, life

In other words, compassion offered by the pound contrived

The way a silk stain on a tie reflective of gem stones

One breathes upon during round three of the pulse taking, through-

Put genuflection tentatively fastened to a formed

Sludge matches scuff points ratcheted up in tandem with one

Or another toy thrown into play pen mentality

Overt as trolls beneath two not-yet-constructed bridges

Imagined before being brought to bear on stamina

Corraled into substantial place because the icicles

Are huge even this afternoon when pale barometers

Of sun disperse a strict light over fringes of the spawned

Clay first moist then saturated before facsimiles

Of heat that coalesce into tuned punctuality

Astigmatic overtones clash with the sideways view of

Trees, discernment happens to peremptory enlargements

Of the kitty previously full of tension and

Impactful fertile traces placed lengthwise across wide town

Matterhorns stochastic as the infraction stowaway

Stalling for impure forms of *tiempo*, flattered by sent

Offerings perchance to sanction utterance, identified

By lotion in the grass beyond our grasp, connected to

Prime numbers left on hold, formed into joy lawns fortified

By advocacy that seems partially substantial in

The text, the trees, the blockwatch obfuscation timed to match

Anarchic potency by six points or perhaps twelve

Remaining alterations crafted into tacit

Worthwhile eminence assigned the weathered apt *fortuna*

Stems of it will bend while branches soften from first-go west

Of database, the mind will plex its way, altruistic

In its line of questioning, live strength pasteurizes depth

Tough to the touch, being ultra careful with exteriors

Sewn to the rigor of a landslide probability

Frost-minted as the charity becomes composed of pine

Pliant to the fine reception in this coated room strewn

With caliber and calibration living amid trees

Three times resilient to anticipated progeny

Absorbent with the sun against the walls inside and out

Trespassing defined by the identity of presence

Majestic, tuned on fire in shards crustacean or deprived

Of necessary walls included in a finished face

Assorted vigor as portrayed on placards won't retreat

The games' proliferate ascendancy unless the sound

Card fails with dance transcendent with domain-fueled positrons

Corroborative and clocked to mean light is epoxy

All the while and quarter tones might pass faculty countdown

Geared to instigate capacity of subtraction in

Unflappable ways new only to the rooks on board spurned

Vessels sharply turned toward the direction of the skid

Where seamless referees punt at the rafters mimicking

Endorsement of whatever passes an inspective tinge

Of eagerness sailing with the plucked strings of a cabin-

Optimal erection of a shelter pacific and

Estranged by lack of use, mere mention of Paul Hindemith

Whose pragmatic urgency inspires such execution

Quite the list man, dowdy though, late fifties early sixties

With a flair for how the language glows when left alone

Both gems and whiskers of detritus splayed to tousled droves

Of pictogranules left to drop derivations in due course

Following a challenge under duress implanted in

A cool heart, is there a blessing to be surreptitious

In a dram's worth of interpretive resurgence wafted in-

To temple tresses caustic seized by watch light sullen waste

And drama ranging high to low in simple droplets crossed

With longhand flow to whisper tense, to shout deceptive dross

Soprano-alto-tenor-bass, conductor-led, contained

By aspects of the tremolo enclosed within the lark

Swift or attuned to featherish soon branches withering

In salt perfume given by water from the sea released

Mobility's another word for dance light skittering

Across a glossy room, a membrance of which sanctifies

What appeared merely a thinly veiled indifference to

Sapling vacuum that punctuates the torsion furnished

By continued stretch goals dominating consciousness or

Striating urgency into several strong strands terse

In their determinate *interpretario* or worse

The furlongs of neural gravity to which one aspires

In tense uncivil ways, the Capricorn commitment lessened

By perceived contrivance center core planted in templates

Capped off by deciduous leaf trickles fast fallen to

Lashes of lawn washed once and then neglected randomly

The lack of recreation showing in the eyesight of

This many decedents known for their ubiquity

Three pieces of something in a row just right for paintbrush

Sketchpad, or lined paper, camera, the pure eye taking

Solace from filled space intending to convey the sense of

Something full not dangerous especially, resembling

White petals plucked from a neighbor's yard and placed in a rinsed bowl

Belonging to oneself and left to change the room with warmth

Contentment other adjectives that half communicate

The speech potential of a lifted rose the color peach

Or nearly captive in a clear bowl that shows the stems and

Thorns as fractions of a system that defines a rose in

Process or in bloom, suffice it to say ready to be

Held at centers multiple and then allowed to raise life

To a higher thought indebted to erase less vital

Thinking about norms, captive sagacity and playthings

What of the cup is pure, what smooth opening obscures white

Meaning a color loses capacity to contain

Locked from the inside formally a mystery puzzling

To all but the overriding mind habitually

Endorsed by its own history, supposing present tense

Will not be anymore a tulip than a sponge taking

With it everything relaxed that can be moved apart

Proximity reputed to be soffit-like plussing

The pure space of inclusion, think of no color at all

Emotion follows mental suit, estrangement captivates

Imagination liquid as a furled flag engaged with

Atmosphere, consider shapeless mental hemp elusive

As the place requiring bandages but free of wood

Or metal or catastrophe lacking fragrance once touched

Rhyme scheme chiseled out of confidence resembles often

Latticed retro- permanence, Apollonian in shades

As corniced as the natural light on shells tuned to fine

Holdings located not made of stiff indulgence, so far

Plant status limited only by seeming repartee

Firm as points along delivery routes etched in mind

Perhaps poised the way we auto harp on themes known as free

Penchants for traveling to Italy in confidence

Beheld as objects lifted to the candlelight and frayed

Open to interpretation, swollen with dampness frilled

Toward arpeggios that lift some sturdy alibis

Recited by authorities refraining from contrived

Speech frosted after being seasoned French as any one

Stunned *langue* easy to come by as perceived sprung near the throng

The glock is twice the rock and roll dyspepsia, for now

Hilltops preside over the rolling causally trained

To-be-adjusted-for deflationary Capricorn

Denomination perplex, chlorine seems not enough some-

Times falling off the hillsides when accomplishment remains

A theory of captivity to which each endurance

Chains its instance to philanthropy to gain credit not

Yet earned as if (repeat) as if the wherewithal were owned

To make a capability be less hamstrung, thus less

Apt to spring into conviction term-limited and stuffed

Into a satchel someplace hidden as true feelings of

A gender constantly unnamed yet porous as the speech

Goes into something like production surfacing not once

But as a matter of due course endeavoring to march

Clarinet miffs music into hutch-like homes, adjusted

Faith-based publicity inherent in right-justified

Stigmatic Fresno where the mother works and Miss Movie

Mis-rehearsed finds judicious creases in the landscape filed

Under obbligato, bonified magna chart's toned

Correspondence course in claustrophia wetted down

By liters of Jack Daniels in a septic copter of

Phlebitis corresponding to a spectacle of plight

And dust-baked hibernation where the sword is healed, rumored

To be true against the granular invective that slights

Factual renditions of routine, a faculty of

Noise denominate and strained, a fourteen-yard penury

Reputed to be worth its weight in loyalty to be

Appropriated as the lawmakers see fit today

House frames an hypothesis that kismet lasts beyond faith

The trees lean over a design that activates our sleep

Then timing challenges a permanence agreed upon

While still the question yet propped open hovers sans response

What has the capacity to enclose decision points

Or difference or threatened everlasting value poised

To trace by finger the endorphins rumored to outlast

Sensation as one crawls across a hardwood floor with light

Scampering over wholeness unbidden where we pounce on

Probability assumed to refute the names of trees

Their temperatures against my skin, the slope of over-

Hanging trees that formed an arch of protection tilled for luck

As folk apprenticed for the moment walled across events

That turned into apologies when wind occurred at last

Farmers will not grow poppies now, the proletariat

Excurses voice majestic as the fated pearl earning

Entire sentences of rest bedazzled by an excess

Of activity intentionally pruned from childhood

As *lederhosen* simplify entanglement just once

The sieve releasing repertoire from tea stains and castors

Plaited tones left in lanes, hair fallen on unnamed tower

Identity patches point and click remuneration

The way mother used to fake most serious breaches of

Austerity and glib-lined reasons for dividing plans

Into foreign and domestic tresses rumored to be

Tranquil at a distance, form the tuning fork of lessons

Lofty in the bait place where the fish won't segregate selves

From nutritional immodesty enlarged to cell size